Probate Possibilities

By Stacy Kellams

WARNING!

REPRODUCTION OF THESE COPYRIGHTED PRINTED MATERIALS ARE PROHIBITED BY LAW.

COPYRIGHT

TRADEMARKS

Company names and product names mentioned in this document are trademarks or registered trademarks of their respective owners and are hereby acknowledged.

LEGAL DISCLAIMER

I am not an attorney and you should seek the advice of a legal professional if you have specific legal questions regarding your state's practices. This training manual is based on Texas law and the Texas system. Other states may be different, but the overall process is the same. Each individual state and furthermore each individual county handles probate a little differently.

PUBLICATION DISCLAIMER

Probate Possibilities assumes no responsibility for errors, inaccuracies, or omissions that may appear in this publication. Probate Possibilities reserves the right to change this publication at any time without notice. This publication is not to be construed as conferring by implication, estoppels, or otherwise any license or right under copyright or patent whether or not the use of any information in this publication employs material claimed in any copyrighted work or an invention claimed in any existing or later issued patent.

Pumpjack Publishing
COPYRIGHT © 2014

Table of Contents

Introduction ……………………………......vii

Dedication ……………………………….x

Chapter 1 ……………………..……1

    Advantages to Probate ………….......1

        Why Probate ……………….1

        Goals …………………….3

Chapter 2 ………………………….4

    Probate 101 ...…………………4

        Probate Process Overview …….4

        Key Players……………….....12

        Probate Treasures …………...13

Chapter 3 …………………………15

    Investing Systems Overview …………...15

        Four Step Investing System…...15

        5 Additional Methods ………...17

Chapter 4 …………………………20

    Probate Notices …………...……….20

        Finding the Notices …………...20

        Reading the Notices ………...22

Chapter 5 ………………...………...27

    Property Search ……...………...…27

        Assessing Real Property……...31

        Probate Worksheet …………...31

        Refining Search …………...…32

Chapter 6 …………………………34

    Probate File …………………36

Application for Probate 36

Death Certificate 39

The Will 39

The Order 42

The Oath 43

The Inventory 44

Chapter 7 46

Contacting the PR 46

Letter Campaign .....…….......46

Phone Contact 47

The Appointment 51

Exhibits If You ordered the Exhibits, they have already arrived via email.

If you did not order the exhibits and would like to order the exhibits, the worksheets and the sample letters for your campaign. CLICK HERE

Exhibit A – Personal Representative Duties

Exhibit B – Classified Ads Webpage

Exhibit C – Probate Notice

Exhibit D – Probate Notice

Exhibit E – Tax Assessor Property Info

Exhibit F – Tax Assessor Property Info

Exhibit G – Application for Probate

Exhibit H – Death Certificate

Exhibit I – The Will

Exhibit J – The Order

Exhibit K – The Oath

Exhibit L – The Inventory

Worksheets
       Life Goals Worksheet
       Probate Worksheet
       Phone Script
       Property Analysis Worksheet
       Comparables Worksheet
       Personal Property Inventory Worksheet

Letter Campaign

Action Item

Your first action item is to write down your goals and what your motivation is for investing in my system. I want you to be honest with yourself and ask yourself what it is that you would like to achieve from this program.

INTRODUCTION

I bought my first investment property back in 1995. I was 25 years old at the time and had just finished reading *Nothing Down* by Robert G. Allen. I was completely new to the real estate business, so a lot of the book was over my head.

It was talking about RAP's and assumable mortgages; I didn't even know what a mortgage was back then. But the one thing that it did do is it motivated me! I went out there and made a deal happen. I found a small deal and I asked the seller if he would owner finance with no money down. He agreed and I was on my way.

Over the past several years I have done everything from rehabs to foreclosures to REO's and short sales. I have wholesaled and retailed. I've done multi-family and mobile homes. I also have a very nice portfolio of rental properties. You name it, I've done it. There is not a whole lot that I haven't seen.

Due to the increasing competition back then, I started looking for a way that I could carve out a niche and do something that no one else was doing. I started trying to figure out how I could set myself apart from all the investors who were plastering bandit signs on telephone poles and street corners and all of the We Buy Houses ads in the newspaper. Then by accident, I stumbled across my first probate deal and knew that that was it, that was my niche.

Let me tell you a little bit about that first probate deal. One day a Personal Representative of an estate called me. She said she had spoken to every investor in town and they had all turned her down. No one could help her.

I decided to meet her at the property and man, this house was in terrible shape. It literally needed $30,000 in repairs. There were also six heirs and no money left to make the mortgage payments. They had run out of funds and the bank had started the foreclosure process. So, the combination of the repairs, the foreclosure, and the probate process had all of the other investors running from this deal.

The property had an ARV (After Repaired Value) of $80,000. They owed $40,000 and it needed $30,000 in repairs. That means you would be in the deal for at least $70,000 and that is why most investors walked away.

So I decided to have them deed me the house, and I sold it a week later for $55,000 without repairs. I was able to sell it to a gentleman who was a contractor and wanted to live in the house and do the repairs himself.

I made a quick $15,000 for one week of work and I said to myself, "Self, there might be something to this probate stuff." The thing that really stuck in my mind about this deal was the fact that every other investor wouldn't touch it. This deal changed my life and I haven't looked back since.

Dedication

As with everything I do in my life, I devote it to my "WHY." My family is WHY I work so hard. Hilary is literally the woman behind this man; her hand on each accomplishment. She is there every day with her intelligence, insight, support, encouragement, faith, her belief in me and her love. We are parenting partners to our three bright and beautiful children, Cage, Caston and Jamesyn.

Chapter 1
Advantages to Probate

With all of the different ways out there to purchase and invest in real estate, why choose probate? The answer is simple; probate is the easiest way to purchase real property and personal property below market value.

Why Probate?

To start with there are ten times more probates than foreclosures in the country and most real estate investors have no idea how to find properties this way. At any given time there are approximately 4 million active probates in the U.S.; that is $6 trillion dollars worth of assets! In addition to that, 1.5 million new active probates come into the system each year, so as you can see there is definitely no shortage of probates.

No competition. Very few investors are actively pursuing probates. I've always lived by this philosophy in life: "If you want to catch a big fish; you need to fish in a pond where no one else is fishing." I've never liked doing exactly the same thing as everyone else, so when the masses are zigging, I try to zag.

One of the reasons there is not a lot of competition in probate is that probate scares most investors. Some investors do not like the idea of purchasing property that is coming out of an estate because obviously someone has just passed away and the idea of that is a little unsettling to them.

I look at it a little bit differently. My view is that we are doing the estate and the Personal Representative of the estate a great service. The Personal Representatives for the estates are completely overwhelmed having been thrust into this position in most cases and we can come in and help settle the estate by taking the real estate off their hands and giving them cash for a quick sale.

Another reason probate scares most investors is because they have a misconception of it being too complex since it deals with the legal system. And while there are legal technicalities, I've cut straight through the complexities and have made them simple and easy to understand. I'm going to show you that this is truly a simple process when you get down to the nuts and bolts of it all.

Another great thing about probate is that you are usually dealing with an unemotional sale. By that I mean, the heirs want the money, not the house. So while yes there are emotions that a loved one has just passed away, they still realize that in order to move forward they have to sell the house, which in turn means you are dealing with motivated sellers! And since we are dealing with motivated sellers, we can buy property all day long for seventy cents on the dollar or less!

Another reason we love probate is because the estate will owner finance properties 50% of the time. That makes it much easier for us to buy these properties because a proportion of our financing is already in place.

With probate it doesn't matter if you're in a good or a bad market. You could be in the worst market in the country in terms of falling prices and slow sales, and it doesn't matter. Probates are in every city in the country because unfortunately, death is unavoidable and it happens in every city throughout the world.

It also doesn't matter if you live in a small town or a large town; if you choose to do this part-time or full-time. You are really getting in on the ground floor, because over the next ten years or so, there is going to be the largest transfer of wealth in the history of the world and it is currently taking place from the Baby Boomers' parents. The Baby Boomers are already the wealthiest class of people to ever walk the face of the earth and they are about to receive even more wealth from their parents.

Goals

I want you to take a minute to think of your current position: personally, professionally, and financially. Now I want you to determine where you would like to be. Setting your goals is absolutely key to your success in any new venture you embark upon.

It has been proven that people who write down their goals and motivating factors for doing something will have 90% more success and will reach their goals faster than someone who does not. The reason most people never reach their goals is because they don't even know what they are!

I have created a Life Goals Worksheet, located in the Worksheets Section of this manual, for you to track your goals along the way. You will want to make sure that you utilize this form, because it is a very important step in achieving your goals.

I want you to remember that everybody needs a why for what they are doing.
It is not important enough to just say, "I want a lot of money." Why do you want a lot of money? That doesn't mean a lot. Why do you want the money? Do not just write down your goals but get to the "whys" behind those goals.

My family is my "why". They are the driving factor behind everything that I do, so I can spend more quality time with them, and real estate has allowed me to do this.

Chapter 2
Probate 101

Now you don't have to be an expert on probate to succeed as an investor, however familiarizing yourself with the basic probate system is vital. Also, the more familiar you become with the process, the more you are able to help the Personal Representatives (from now on we'll call them the PRs) when they contact you and that is what it is all about, helping the PRs help you. The more knowledgeable you are and the more willing you are to help, the better your chances of building a rapport with the PR and closing a deal.

Probate Process Overview

Probate is the legal process by which a person's financial debts are settled and legal title to the property is formally passed from the decedent to his or her

beneficiaries/heirs. It is initiated in the county of the
decedent's legal residence at the time of death.
Somebody acting on behalf of the decedent must come
forward with the decedent's original will. Usually, this
person is named in the will as the executor, chosen by
the decedent as the one in charge of "wrapping up" his
or her affairs.

The probate process typically begins within thirty days
of the decease of the individual, but there are exceptions.
State statute indicates an amount of time by which the
process must start. In other words, an estate cannot
typically be probated two hundred years after the
deceased has died (if there were such a situation a court
other than one of probate would likely be involved). For
example, under Texas probate law, the decedent's will
must be probated within 4 years of decedent's passing.

The following are the general steps in the process. After
the decedent passes away, he or she leaves behind his or
her estate. The "estate" is everything that the decedent
owned at the time of his or her death. The estate is
broken into two categories: real property and personal
property. Real property refers to the real estate which
would be any land and/or buildings. Personal property is
a specific legal term referring to anything that is not real
estate; e.g. cash, a computer, furniture, shares of stock,
an IRA account, and so forth.

Then we have the will. If the decedent had a valid will, then he or she is said to have died testate. If the decedent did not have a will, then he or she is said to have died intestate.

If there is a will, the named executor will bring it before the court that handles probates in the jurisdiction. Witnesses then may testify that they were at the execution of the document. Not all wills are determined to be valid and the court may proceed as if the decedent left no will at all.

If there is no will and the decedent passed away intestate, the estate will pass through to the heirs according to the laws of descent in the decedent's state of residence. Each state and/or county has its own laws regarding what happens when there is no will, so you will need to do some research to find out exactly what your state and county laws are.

Then you have the court process to appoint a Personal Representative. If the personal representative named in the will agrees to administer the estate, his appointment is made official by the court so he can carry out the terms of the will. Once the PR is appointed by the court, he or she has the authority to deal with the assets of the estate.

The "probate court" may actually be called the probate court in your county or the probate may be handled by the county court or district court. Some states call their courts by another name, such as the superior court, and probates are handled in those courts. We'll refer to them generally as the probate court for now. Because probate courts are state courts and not federal courts, the process they follow may vary from one state to another. Yet despite their differences, these courts all pretty much follow the same basic process, which can be divided into three steps:

1. Collection, inventory, and appraisal of all assets that are subject to probate.

   One of the PR's first and most important duties after appointment is to take an inventory of the estate's assets. These assets include money that is owed to the decedent or the estate, e.g. loans, final paycheck, life insurance, or retirement account made payable to the estate. Generally, this inventory must be filed with the court.

If the decedent's property contains bank and stock brokerage accounts, the bank or brokerage firm name and the balances on the date of decedent's passing would be listed. Valuing real estate or an antique car collection, by contrast, would probably require a professional appraisal. The professional valuation of an asset and the detail included in the inventory are generally dictated by the court, but may also be influenced by the size of the estate or the degree of scrutiny being shown by other interested parties.

2. Paying the bills – taxes, estate expenses, and creditors of the decedent.

The PR reviews the decedent's final bills, debts, and any claims against him or her as well as the supporting proof. The PR then pays or settles those that are valid and rejects the rest. He or she may hire an attorney with estate funds for advice, to defend, or negotiate any legal claims. The law requires that all creditors of the decedent have notice and a chance to present their claims. A publication notice is then published in the paper indicating that the estate is being probated and that claims against the estate should be filed within a specific amount of time. The order of payment of claims against the estate is usually:

1. Costs/expenses of Administration
2. Funeral expenses
3. Debts and taxes
4. All other claims

What most people do not realize is that once someone passes away, all of their assets are technically frozen for a period of time because the decedent is no longer around and there is generally no one with any legal authority to handle these assets. The PR then has to go through the probate process to get them unfrozen. However, the decedent's creditors still have the expectation that they will be paid even during the period of time when the assets are frozen. When someone passes away, their debts are not just forgiven. The mortgage still has to be paid along with all of the other bills. Where is that money going to come from if all of the assets are frozen? Most often it is coming from the PR's own pocket.

3. Formal transfer of estate property according to the will or by the state laws of intestate succession (if there is no will).

When all rightful claims, debts, and expenses have been paid, the remainder of the property is distributed by the executor as the will directs. (At this point, if there is no will, the PR distributes the property according to state law.) The PR generally has the discretion to distribute the estate in cash or in kind (give away the property itself; for example, give the car to beneficiary Sally instead of giving her the cash from the sale

of the car), but the will may
specify otherwise.

If the will permits it, the PR may
sell or transfer real estate when the
timing is right in the administration
of the estate. The PR usually may
sell or transfer the decedent's
personal property any time but
may not begin final distribution of
property and sale proceeds until
after a waiting period provided by
state law.

When the waiting periods have
expired and the legitimate bills,
debts, and taxes have been paid,
what remains of the estate is
available for distribution to
beneficiaries/heirs. Only then may
the PR make disbursements of cash
or transfer physical property to the
respective beneficiaries/heirs.

A final settlement or accounting is generally required of
all the PR's dealings on behalf of the estate. Any party
who intends to object to any aspect of the probate
proceedings should come forward and be heard at this
point if not sooner. Once the judge approves the final

settlement, the PR usually has no further duties, and the estate no longer exists.

The Key Players

Let's talk about the key players. First we have the deceased or the decedent. You cannot have a probate until someone passes away.

Then you have the beneficiaries or the heirs. A beneficiary is a person, related or not, whom the decedent has specifically named in either a will, insurance policy, trust, survivorship agreement or other contract, to be the taker of his or her property. An heir is any of the decedent's relatives who would be in line under state law to take a part of the decedent's estate if he or she died without a will.

The Personal Representative, otherwise known as the PR, is the Executor if male or Executrix if female. They could also be called the Administrator if male or the Administratrix if female. Now, most wills are drafted with the general term Executor and typically you will not hear the female versions, but I still wanted to make you aware of them incase you happen to run across them.

The PR is going to be your main point of contact, since they handle all of the matters of the estate and are the ones who have direct contact with the attorney. They have a very long list of duties they must perform (see Exhibit A) in addition to their everyday lives and jobs. In most cases they are paid very little and in some cases they are not paid at all.

Then there is the Probate Attorney. The attorney works for the estate and advises the PR; however they are not the final decision maker. A lot of people get scared because they think that they are going to have to deal with attorneys. In reality, that is only the case if the attorney happens to be the PR and I usually try and avoid that situation.

We also have the Probate Records Clerks. They are the people down at your local county probate courthouse and they are the gatekeepers of the probate information world. You want to be very, very nice to these people. They are overworked and underpaid and they hold all of the pertinent information that you will need to access. I highly suggest taking them cookies, cakes, learning their first names, finding out their birthdays, etc. You are truly going to want to befriend these people. They can help you or they can hinder you.

Probate Treasures

Personal property is a hidden treasure in probate. Even though this system is specifically for real estate investing, I wanted to touch on the additional profits that you can make with personal property as well.

Personal property, like I mentioned before, is all the personal possessions (not real estate) the decedent owned at the time of his or her death; for example, furniture, cloths, jewelry, collectables, tools, cars, etc.

Just like the real estate, most of these possessions will be sold to settle the estate and just like real estate you can pick-up these possessions for pennies on the dollar. Since you are usually the first on the scene to purchase the real estate, you can let the PR know upfront that you may be interested in some of the personal property as well, giving you first pick.

A lot of the probates you will handle will be for elderly individuals and their personal property often includes great antiques. For anyone who is ever watched the TV program Antique Roadshow, I'm sure you can understand how valuable some personal property can be.

After you purchase items, you can turn around and resell them at estate sales, online auctions or antique retailers. With eBay growing each year it is the perfect place to list these items for sale. A lot of people make a very good living off of selling items on eBay and now you can get in on the action too! You may also choose to keep certain items for your own personal use.

Chapter 3
Investing Systems Overview

There are several ways in which you can purchase probate property. The system that I use is by far the best way to get in early and eliminate the competition. However, there are some additional methods to purchasing probate property that I will also go over very briefly.

Four Step Investing System

Now I have broken my system down into four simple steps. Here is a quick overview of what we will be discussing in the next several chapters.

> Step 1: The very first thing that you have to do is find the name and the case number of the deceased in your

local newspaper or legal publication. This is the most important step, because without it you're dead in the water. You have to find where your legal notices and/or probate notices are published in your local area.

Step 2: After you have found the decedent's name and case number, the next step is to find out if they owned any real estate. If they didn't own real estate, you are going to want to move on to the next case. So we must first determine whether they owned any real property through your local tax assessor's office.

Step 3: You need to find the name and address of the Personal Representative. Many times the PR is listed in the probate notice; however, you will generally have to get his or her address from the probate file that you will obtain from the county clerk's office.

Step 4: You are going to send a letter campaign to the PR and you are going to make a deal!

That's it, those are the four steps. You can cut through everything else and boil it down to those in my investing system.

Throughout this manual, I am going to be covering everything from A to Z. However, I don't want you to get bogged down in all of the legalities, terms, documents, and so forth. I am going to show you how to cut through it all so that you can pick out the most vital information that you will need to get the best deal as quickly as possible.

A lot of the information that I will be giving you may seem irrelevant to making money with this system; however, it is just like back in school when you had to learn how to do long division by hand and the teacher wouldn't let you use a calculator. You have to learn it the long way first before you can skip straight to the short cut. All the information is important so that you become comfortable with what you are looking at and looking for.

5 Additional Methods

Like I said before, this manual is how to purchase probate properties using my 4 step system. However, there are five additional methods of purchasing probate property that you need to be aware of as well.

1. Buying Probate Property at a Public Auction

A public auction is usually held by the attorney for the estate in which potential buyers place an oral bid on the property and the attorney acts as the auctioneer. The highest bid of course wins.

These auctions are published in the newspaper with the address of the property to be auctioned.

2. Buying Probate Property at a Private Auction

A private auction is generally held with a professional real estate auction company in which buyers orally bid on the property and the highest bid wins.

The auction company will usually send out fliers and emails to their customer list. I would highly recommend locating your local auction company and signing up to get on their list.

3. Buying Probate Property at a Private Sale

A private sale is usually held by the attorney of the estate in which potential buyers submit a sealed bid to the attorney. The highest bid wins.

These auctions are published in the newspaper with the attorney's contact information.

4. Buying Probate Property from Trust Departments

In certain situations a trust department of a bank can be an executor to an estate. When this happens they take on all of the responsibilities of the executor which includes selling the real property.

Call the bank for a list of the properties they currently have available in probate.

5. Buying Probate Property from Agents

In some cases, the executors don't know any other way to sell the property so they immediately enlist the services of a real estate agent as soon as they are able to sell the property. Unfortunately, this is probably your least likely place to get a good deal since the agents usually take the great deals before they go on the market.

Chapter 4
Probate Notices

Finding the probate notices is the most vital step of the
system. Typically, they are not published in the main
daily newspaper. The attorneys have to run the Notice to
Creditors (a.k.a. - probate notice) three times within a 10
day period. They usually don't run them in the
mainstream paper because it's prohibitively expensive.
You will most likely find them located in the smaller,
less known papers with more local circulation. If you
are in a large city your area may have a legal publication
or legal newspaper where all the legal notices are
printed.

Finding the Notices

There are three ways you can find where the legal
notices are published. First, contact your daily
newspaper. Let them know you are specifically looking

for the probate notices and would like to know where they are published.

Second, contact your County Probate Court. The people in the courthouse have a wealth of information and knowledge. However, it is best that you visit in person instead of simply calling.

Third, contact a local probate attorney's office. When you call their office you are obviously not going to get an attorney on the phone. However, more often than not, the receptionist or the legal secretary will know where they file them and may be more helpful.

Most newspapers are online now and due to that, you can most often search the probate notices for free on the internet. For example (see Exhibit B), this is a print out of the Austin Chronicle, my local secondary newspaper, classified ads webpage. If you look down at the bottom under Neighborhood you will see the Legal section. This is what you are looking for. Again your local publications may be just a little bit different, but the overall fundamentals are the same. The estate generally chooses one publication to list the notices in; however they could run them in several, that is up to the estate. So you will need to check all publications with legal notices in your area.

Reading the Notices

When you are looking through your local publications, there are several ways that a Probate Notice could be listed, for example: Notice to Creditors, Citation of Publication, Estate Notices, Notice to All Persons, etc. Let me take a minute to explain what some of these terms mean.

> Citation of Publication – It is the first required posting to begin the probate. It is posted in a paper of general circulation in the county in which the deceased was domiciled (where the deceased lived at the time of his or her death).

> Notice to Creditors – This can also be listed as Notice to All Persons, Notice to All and Published Notice to Creditors. This is a required posting after the PR is appointed by the court. The purpose of this posting is to serve as notice to anyone, i.e. creditors or anyone else that may have a claim against the estate, that they need to submit the claim to the estate within a specific time period, also called the statutory time. Most states have a law

that requires the creditor to submit a
claim by the allotted time or the claim
will be dismissed.

Letters Testamentary – This is issued
by the court when the decedent had a
will. This document is evidence that
the probate court has appointed the
person named in the letters
testamentary to be the independent
executor of the estate with full
authority to act on behalf of the estate.

Here is an example of a probate notice in my area (see
Exhibit C if you purchased the Exhibits. If not, see Table
of Contents to order). It reads, "The State of Texas to
All Persons Interested in the Estate of Magdalene M.
Reid, Deceased, No. 87,184 in Probate Court Number
One of Travis County, Texas. Michael Larnell Bexley
alleged heir(s) at law in the above numbered and entitled
estate, filed on the 6th day of August, 2007, an
Application to Determine Heirship in the said estate and
request(s) that the said Court determine who are the heirs
and only heirs of the said Magdalene M. Reid, Deceased,
and their respective shares and interests in such estate."

Now, how much information did we get from that
notice? We found out the deceased's name, Magdalene

M. Reid, and the case number, No. 87,184. This is the number that you will need when you go down to the courthouse to access the deceased's probate file. We also have the name of the potential Personal Representative, Michael Larnell Bexley, because he is the one who filed the application to determine heirship.

Here is another example of a probate notice (see Exhibit D if you purchased the Exhibits. If not, see Table of Contents to order). It reads, "The State of Texas to All Persons Interested in the Estate of Norman James Burlingame, Deceased, No. 87,178 in Probate Court Number One of Travis County, Texas. Judith Alice Burlingame, a.k.a. Judith LaPolt Burlingame, alleged heir(s) at law in the above numbered and entitled estate, filed on the 3rd day of August, 2007, an Application to Determine Heirship and for issuance of Letters of an Independent Administration in the said estate and request(s) that the said Court determine who are the heirs and only heirs of said Norman James Burlingame, Deceased, and their respective shares and interests in such estate."

You can see in the notice that it states "alleged heir(s)" which means that either the decedent did not have a will or that it is unclear who the beneficiaries of the estate are. It also states that they are requesting the Issuance of Letters of an Independent Administration which indicates that all heirs are know, but that the decedent did not have a will.

The fact that they are requesting Issuance of Letters of an Independent Administration means that the person appointed by the court will have the authority to act on behalf of the estate without having to ask for the court's permission. This is great news because the less court involvement the better. It will make the deal run much smoother with minimum court involvement.

I also wanted to clarify that although the notice states that a hearing will be held at 10:00 a.m. on the first Monday following the expiration of ten days from the date of the Publication of Citation, this is not necessarily the actual time of the hearing. For instance, in Travis County, the uncontested determination of heirship cases are heard on Tuesday morning between 8:30 a.m. and 10:00 a.m. each week.

Uncontested means the heirs/beneficiaries of the estate do not have any objections in the case. If it is a contested case it means that there are objections and in that case you would not want to get involved. However, most will not be contested.

So you can see there is a lot of information to be found just in the probate notice. Again, that is why this step is so important. Next, we want to see if the deceased owned any real property at the time of his or her death.

Action Item

Your next action item is to find the probate notices in your local area. I have given you three helpful steps in doing so, but if you are still having problems locating them then try doing a Google search as well.

Chapter 5
Property Search

Now I am going to show you how to take the information that we have gathered from the probate notice and use that information to determine whether the deceased actually owned any real estate.

First, you will need to do a Google search to find your local county tax assessor's website. If you are unable to locate it online you may need to call their office and ask them for their web address.

If they are not online, that means you are going to have to go down and do a physical search on their computers in their office. Don't worry. This means that in order for anybody to do a search in your particular county; they have to go down to the tax assessor's office as well.

That raises what I call, "The pain in the butt factor." If "The pain in the butt factor" goes up for you, it goes up for everyone. Now most people won't jump through very many hoops. They are looking for the easiest deal possible and that means even less competition for you.

Once you have located your tax assessor's website, you are going to want to do a search for Real Property by Owners name, which would be the decedent's name. Do not put the first name or middle initial in the search, just the last name. You want to see everything that is listed on the tax rolls and the first and middle initial can differ depending on how they listed their name. Of course, if you have a name like Smith there is going to be several listings, so you will want to narrow it down in that case.

Assessing Real Property

First of all, we need to narrow down the search to the decedents that have real property only. We want to know which estates we want to pursue with the greatest likelihood of letting us pick up the property for 70 cents on the dollar or less.

I'm going to continue to use the last probate notice (Exhibit D) as an example in the property search. My local tax assessor is the Travis County Appraisal District. After doing a quick search for Burlingame I have two properties come up under a Norman J. and

Judith Burlingame. If we refer back to the probate notice, the name of the alleged heir is Judith.

That tells us right off the bat that we are probably dealing with a surviving spouse. Once I click through to the tax appraisal rolls (see Exhibit E), I see the address is 2615 Rainfall Trail Cedar Park, Texas. We now know that yes, Norman did own real estate and the surviving spouse, Judith, is probably still living in the real estate.

If there is a surviving spouse, you are typically not going to be able to purchase that property. However, that is not always 100% the case. Sometimes the surviving spouse may want to sell the real estate and move in with a child, down grade to something smaller or move to an assisted living home. So if you are limited on leads in your area, you may want to consider moving forward, even if there is a surviving spouse.

We now have the address of the potential investment and can start sending out our campaign letters. We also see the deed date. They purchased the property on 12/18/2000 so that gives us an idea that they have owned the property for seven years and I know that over the last seven years property values have definitely increased here in Austin.

Since they have owned the property for seven years there has been a considerable amount of pay-down on the property and this could mean that they have a substantial amount of equity.

There are a couple of other things to note; over in the right hand corner under Property Details you will see the exemptions and the freeze exemptions. The HS stands for homestead and the F stands for freeze exemption. Your taxing authority might do things a little different but here in Texas, once a person reaches 65 years of age or older, the state limits how high they can raise the taxes. This particular property has an F under exemptions which tells us that we are dealing with someone who is 65 years or older.

Then under the most recent tax year we can see the tax assessed value of the home. However, the tax assessed value is generally not the true market value for the property. The tax assessed value doesn't take into consideration the condition of the property, for example.

We can also see that the house sits on .16 acres, the land value is about $30,000 and the improvement value is $136,000 for a total value around $166,000. We also see that it was built in 1995; it has a first and second floor and is approximately 1,983 square feet. We are getting a lot of good information just by looking at the tax appraisal roll.

Probate Worksheet

This is where we are going to start inputting all of our vital information that we have gathered from the probate notice and the tax assessor's property information.

Please refer to the Probate Worksheet in the Worksheet Section of this Manual (if you purchased the Exhibits and worksheets. If not, see the Table of Contents to order). Starting at the top of the Probate Worksheet you can see there is a space for the decedent's name where it says Estate of ____.

Directly below that, we have a section for the Executor's information. It is conveniently placed at the top where it is easy to see, since as I have stated before they will be your main point of contact.

Below that, there is a section for the Subject Property, which would obviously be the property we are intending to purchase.

Over to the side, you have a section for the Court Information and Tracking Dates.

And then at the very bottom of the page, you have the Heirs Information and Additional Notes.

This should be pretty self explanatory. Just fill in the information required.

Refining Search

Since the last property search most likely has a surviving spouse, I'm going to go to my next probate notice here for the Estate of Ruby Flow. When I entered her last name into the TCAD (Texas County Appraisal District), I find that there are two Flows listed and the second one is a Ruby K. Flow.

Once I click through to her Property Information (see Exhibit F), I can see that she does own real property with an assessed value of $154, 541.

Now something interesting I instantly see is that the mailing address is in Del Valle, Texas, which is not the address of the property. We have a mailing address that is different than the address of the property. That tells us that the tax bill is going somewhere else, which means that the decedent was most likely not residing at the homestead. And since there is an F under the exemptions, we know that the decedent was over 65 years of age.

Based on the information so far, I definitely want to investigate this one further. So now I'm going to go over to my Probate Worksheet and I'm going to start entering in all of the information I have on the Flow estate.

Once I have as much information filled out on the Probate Worksheet that I can, I am then going to go down to the courthouse and pull the actual probate file.

Action Item

Your next action item is to find your local county tax assessor's website and/or office.

Chapter 6
Probate File

Now that we have finished our preliminary searches, we need to finalize our research by finding the actual probate file. This step is going to require you going down to your local Probate County Courthouse. Some of the larger cities may have access to this information online, but it is very unlikely.

Again, don't get discouraged, because that just means that there is going to be less competition. Remember what I said, if you have to take an extra step then that means everybody has to take that extra step as well.

Now remember what I said before, it is always a good idea to be very nice to the people working in the clerk's office. One way to do this is to avoid going in to do your research on their busiest days of the week.

For instance, here in my county the new probates must be filed by Thursday at 4:00 p.m. to be added to the list for required notices and to be added to the next court docket. They also hold the majority of their probate hearings on Tuesday and Wednesday mornings.

Therefore, it is best that I avoid the clerk's offices at those times. You do not want to go down there and have to wait in line or add any additional stress to the people in the clerk's offices already hectic day. I generally do my research on Fridays because that is their least busy day. I suggest that you research your clerk's office and determine the best times for you.

From our probate notice search, we obtained the name of the decedent, the probate case number, and the date that the Letters Testamentary were issued.

We can either use the case number or the decedent's name to search the probate records at the county clerk's office.

Now I want to show you what I found when I went down to my local probate court and pulled the probate file for Ruby Flow. I also want to go through some of the documents that you are going to find in the probate files.

Application for Probate

The first thing that we are going to find is the Application for Probate, which may also be called the Petition for Probate. You can't probate an estate without requesting that the court open a probate file for the estate which must be done through a written application or petition to the court.

Once the application is filed with the court, the court will assign a case number, also referred to as the cause number or docket number. When they assign the case number to a particular probate estate, all the documents filed for the estate will have the case number on them.

Once you become familiar with this process, you will start to notice a system in which the clerk's office numbers their records. You will notice that the system may be that one file will be numbered 86,976 and then the very next file will be 86,977, and so on. The point is, the courthouse is going to be using some numbering system and once you figure out what it is then you may not even need to look up the probate notices anymore because you will be able to go down and ask for the next file in line. This also helps if you are having a hard time locating your probate notices in your local publication.

You will notice that the applicant's name on the application is usually the person who is named as the executor in the will (usually a family member or a close friend). This person is generally the person who hired the attorney to file the necessary probate documents.

Now looking at the Flow Application for Probate (Exhibit G), we can see that Diane Flow Turner is the applicant who furnished the following information to the court in support of the Application for Probate of the written will of Ruby Flow, the decedent, for the issuance of Letters Testamentary.

Let's look at some of the key points of the application. We see that the applicant's middle name is Flow, which is the last name of the decedent. It is a very good possibility that the applicant is related to the decedent and is possibly her daughter.

The application also gives us the address of the applicant, which is the main address where we will want to send our letter campaign since she is most likely the PR. Furthermore, the applicant's address is in a different town and county than the decedent's. This is a good sign, because people will usually not want to deal with property that is not in the same town in which they live.

Continuing on, we can see under Item Number 2 in Exhibit G that the application has the date and time of the decedent's death, as well as her age and what town and county she lived in at the time of death.

Item Number 4 on the application shows a general list of what they believe to be included in the decedent's estate at this time. You can see it includes real property which is exactly what we are looking for. It states that the decedent owned property described generally as real estate, personal property, and household goods of a probable value in excess of $200,000. This is another great sign and the pieces of the puzzle are starting to come together.

In Item Number 7, we see that the decedent was married one time during her lifetime to Edward Thomas Flow. Edward Thomas Flow predeceased the decedent on November 26, 1978. So that tells us that Ruby Flow has been widowed since 1978.

Item Number 8 shows that Ruby Flow did in fact have a will and we can see that she named three people to serve as "Co-Executors" without bond. The three people named are John T. Flow, Diane Flow Turner, and Karol Flow Reinhardt. However, the Application also states that John and Karol have each signed a waiver and renunciation of right to letters testamentary, leaving Diane as the sole Executor.

So putting it all together, we now know that Ruby Flow owned real property at the time of her death and had no surviving spouse. Her daughter isn't living in the house because her address is different than the address of the property. And we know that Diane is the person we are going to want to deal with since she is the sole Executor and is the one that has the authority to settle the estate.

Death Certificate

There will always be a death certificate in the file. There is a lot of the same information on the death certificate as the Application for Probate; however, there is some additional information that we can still obtain.

For instance, (see Exhibit H) it has the address of where the decedent was living at the time of death, which we can see was an assisted living home. That means that the property in question may be vacant, a family member could be living there, or perhaps it is currently being rented.

We also learn that there is a different address listed for Diane Flow Turner than what was listed on the Application for Probate. This is good to know, because when we start to send out our letter campaign, we will want to send the letters to both addresses.

The Will

Wills can differ in many different ways, so I don't want you to get too bogged down with the legal aspect of it.

I'm going to show you how to cut right through it all and get the information that we are looking for.

The Executor is required to follow the decedent's directions regarding the administration and distribution of the decedent's estate as written and provided for in the will, unless otherwise directed by the court.

Article II of the will (see Exhibit I) begins the provisions regarding the distribution of the estate. You can see that all of the decedent's personal effects are to be divided equally among her children and everything else is to go to a specific trust named in the will that was created in 1986. Note that since there is no special provision for real property, any real property that the decedent owned would go into the trust.

Article IV describes what is to happen if the 1986 trust does not exist when the testator dies. If the trust does not exist, then everything, other than the personal property already specifically mentioned in Article II, goes to "those of my descendants that survive me per stirpes." This is just a fancy way of saying that it goes to her three children, but if one of the three children has past away then that child's share is distributed equally to that deceased child's descendants, and if he or she had no descendants, the share would be equally divided among the other two children.

If all of the children of the decedent have past away then the will provides that the estate go to the heirs. The court would then look at her family tree to determine who the heirs would be.

Article V shows who the decedent named as the Independent Co-Executors, which we already have from the Application for Probate. It also states under Item 5.2 that, "no action shall be required in any court in relation to the settlement of my estate other than the probating of my will and the return of an inventory, appraisement and list of claims of my estate." This phrase and the words "Independent Executor" are the wording I look for since it means there will be less court supervision and it ensures that the executor has full authority to act on behalf of the estate.

Also note there is a specific provision stating that the executor shall not receive any compensation for serving under the will. That means that the executor is responsible for all of her duties and responsibilities laid forth in the will but she is not getting paid to do the work --- and trust me, it's a lot of work. That just adds a little more motivation to get the estate settled quickly.

You will also note that the testator, the person who signed the will (now the decedent), wants any taxes due to be paid from the residue of the estate, which includes any real property in this case.

Let's go to Article VII, the fiduciary provisions. This lists all the powers the testator has given the independent executor. In this case the powers granted are very broad and the independent executor can do pretty much anything regarding the property of the estate without court approval.

Article VIII basically states that the beneficiary cannot transfer his interest in the estate before he actually receives the property and the beneficiary's creditors cannot use this interest in the estate to satisfy the beneficiary's debt until the beneficiary actually receives the property.

This Article also states that if any beneficiary is under the age of 21 or incapacitated at the time of the testator's death, the beneficiary's share will be held in trust by the executor until the beneficiary reaches age 21 or capacity. This article also defines what testator means by "descendants and heirs."

The Order

At the end of the probate hearing, the court will issue an order probating the will, or for the administration of the estate if there is no original will, and will issue Letters Testamentary (for an Independent Administration of a will), or Letters of Administration (for an Independent

Administration when there is no will). You may also see
orders for Dependent Administration which means that
the Administrator / Executor (not Independent Executor)
must get court approval before taking any action
regarding the estate. I generally avoid these types of
probate because it is a much slower process.

The order will tell you who the court has appointed as
the Independent Executor and what further actions that
person is required to take with the court.

For instance, you will see the key phrase we are looking
for in the last sentence of Exhibit J, "And no other action
shall be had in this court other than the return of the
inventory, the appraisement and list of claims."

Again, this is just one more piece of evidence that we are
dealing with an independent administration and the PR
has full authority.

The Oath

Each executor must sign an oath that he or she will,
"well and truly perform all the duties of the independent
administrator." This is usually signed at or just
following the probate hearing in the presence of a deputy
or county clerk. (see Exhibit K if you ordered the
Exhibits)

The Inventory

If you are looking at a recent probate, it may not contain an inventory, which was the case with the Flow estate. The inventory is generally due 90 days after the executor is appointed.

Since the Flow estate did not have an inventory, I have pulled an inventory from another file for an example, Exhibit L.

If you take a look at the inventory, you will see again the case number which is assigned to that particular file, the name of the decedent and the court and the county in which it was filed. All of that information is located in the top right hand corner along with the date of death.

Please note the phrase "list of claims" refers to claims owed to the estate, not claims the estate owes someone else. That is a very important distinction. A file for an independent administration will not show the debts the estate must pay.

Texas is a community property state, so the inventory here must designate whether the property listed in the inventory is community property or separate property. And as you can see in Exhibit L, everything is listed as separate property.

I wanted to use this inventory as an example because the decedent had more than just a residence included in the estate. You can tell by the real property listed in Schedule A of the Inventory there was a substantial amount of real estate, including rental property, commercial property and vacant land.

You will also notice on the Inventory that there are no stocks, bonds, mortgages, notes or cash listed. You will see items listed here in most probates. If you don't see any of these items listed on the Inventory, that means the decedent held some or all of these types of assets either in joint accounts with rights of survivorship or in a trust. Both of which are considered non-probate assets and not included in the Inventory.

Do not assume because there are no cash or liquid assets listed in the estate they do not exist. Likely those particular assets did not have to go through the probate process. Ask the PR or heirs about them instead.

Action Item

Pull the probate notices from your local paper and the tax information for the decedents listed in the probate notices. Go down to the courthouse and pull at least one probate file for one of the estates you find with real property and start a probate worksheet.

Chapter 7
Contacting the PR

Letter Campaign

Your first point of contact with the PR will start with a four letter mailing campaign that I have created especially for this manual. You will want to send your first letter in the campaign immediately after pulling the probate file at the courthouse. You are then going to follow up with the second, third and then the fourth letter during the administration of the estate. (See the Letter Campaign Section at the end of this manual.)

It usually takes anywhere between four and seven contacts with somebody before they usually feel comfortable contacting you back. Some won't contact you back at all and that's okay. It is just a numbers game. Some people will and some people won't. You just move onto the next one.

You may live in an area where you do not need to send off four letters. You may only need to send one or two. I will let you be the judge of that. You may be getting enough leads from just one letter or you may have to add a letter to the sequence. The only wrong way to do this is by not doing it at all.

Basically, the mantra that I live by is that, "Letters sent equals money in the bank." The more letters you send, the more money you're going to put in the bank. Again, this is a numbers game.

You want to be consistent and make sure that you are sending your letters every single week. Just designate one day for your letter campaign and stick with it each week. Be persistent and consistent; that is the most important thing. Do not skip a week.

Phone Contact

At some point, you will want to add a phone call to the PR into the sequence. I am going to let you decide where to do that since some people are shyer about talking on the phone and others are more aggressive. Some of the more aggressive people may want to give the PR a phone call before or directly after the first letter and that's okay. There is no right and wrong way to this part of the system. It's all based on personal preference and comfort level.

However, you need to keep in mind that real estate is a people business. It's about people helping people. So at some point, you will ultimately need to get over your shyness and learn to speak with people over the phone and in person.

You want to remember to always be very friendly with the PR. We want to be a friend of the estate, so they know that we are there to answer any questions they may have and to help them in any way possible. You want to create a rapport so that they feel comfortable doing business with you.

Once you have the PR on the phone, you will want to obtain additional information about the property in question.

I have created a phone script (see the Phone Script in the Worksheet Section) for you to use until you get comfortable with asking your own questions.

I do not recommend that you make the PR an offer over the phone before looking at the property. This is an extremely advanced strategy. Even if you are an advanced real estate investor and you have already driven past the property in hopes that the PR was going to contact you, I still think it's better to wait.

Don't forget that there is still a sensitivity factor when dealing with probate properties. It was a loved one's property and the PR most likely has a connection to the property. It would be disrespectful and irresponsible to shoot them a blind offer over the phone.

> Question 1:   The very first thing you want to ask them is, "What are your plans for the property?"

> Obviously, if they've called you then they are probably looking to sell. However, you still want to ask.

> Question 2:   The next thing you want to ask them is, "Are there any repairs that need to be made to the property and if so what is the estimated cost?"

> You want them to start thinking about what's wrong with the property and what repairs, if any, need to be made. Someone's going to have to make those repairs. If they don't want to make the repairs themselves, then they

are going to have to allow for that by reducing the price.

Question 3:   Next you will want to ask, "How much is owed on the property?"

You are basically trying to find out if there is a mortgage or if the property is free and clear.

Question 4:   Then you want to ask them, "What are you going to do if the property doesn't sell?"

That question will give you an idea of what their plans are and how motivated they really are to sell.

Question 5:   You also want to ask them, "How quickly would you like to sell the property?"

Again, this is going to give you a good idea of how motivated they are to sell and how quickly they are looking to do so.

Question 6:   Another question you
will want to ask them is, "Give me an
idea of what you feel the property is
worth in its current condition?"

A lot of them will try to tell you that
it's worth full market value even
though repairs need to be made. Don't
worry about that right now. You can
discuss that with them at a later time.
Right now, we're just building our
rapport and gathering information.

The Appointment

When the PR contacts you, the only thing I want to see
you do after you prescreen the property is to set an
appointment for viewing.

I like to set the appointment for one to two days later.
That allows me time to go back to the courthouse and
pull the file again. By this time, hopefully the inventory
is in the file and they have assessed a value or given a
value to the real estate. This is going to give you a really
good idea about what kind of number the PR has in mind
as to the value of the property.

Now you may be thinking, "Whoa, Stacy, what do you mean wait one to two days? All of the other real estate gurus are telling me to see it that day."

Just remember, they are talking about foreclosure leads. There is so much competition with foreclosures that they are absolutely right. If a foreclosure lead calls you, you better drop what you're doing and get over there right away.

That's not the case with probate. You are probably the first and only person they have contacted, so there isn't a big rush. You do however want to be responsible and ask the PR if you are in fact the only contact for them selling the property at this point and time.

They will be honest with you and if no one else is looking at the property, then there is no reason to rush.

Action Item

I want you to become familiar and comfortable with the phone script. Contact a PR by phone and set an appointment. Then find a local contractor and have them go through the walk through with you to assess the repairs. Have them go through everything they look for and how they arrived at the estimated repairs.